First published in Great Britain in 1996 by
BROCKHAMPTON PRESS,
20 Bloomsbury Street,
London WC1B 3QA.
A member of the Hodder Headline Group,

This series of little gift books was made by Frances Banfield, Andrea P. A.
Belloli, Polly Boyd, Kate Brown, Stefano Carantini, Laurel Clark, Penny Clarke,
Clive Collins, Jack Cooper, Melanie Cumming, Nick Diggory, John Dunne,
Deborah Gill, David Goodman, Paul Gregory, Douglas Hall, Lucinda Hawksley,
Maureen Hill, Dennis Hovell, Dicky Howett, Nick Hutchison, Douglas Ingram,
Helen Johnson, C.M. Lee, Simon London, Irene Lyford, John Maxwell, Patrick
McCreeth, Morse Modaberi, Tara Neill, Sonya Newland, Anne Newman, Grant
Oliver, Ian Powling, Terry Price, Michelle Rogers, Mike Seabrook, Nigel Soper,
Karen Sullivan and Nick Wells.

ISBN 1 86019 4184

A copy of the CIP data is available from the British Library
upon request.

Produced for Brockhampton Press by Flame Tree Publishing, a part
of The Foundry Creative Media Company Limited, The Long House,
Antrobus Road, Chiswick W4 5HY.

Printed and bound in Italy by L.E.G.O. Spa.

Just For You
THANK
YOU

Illustrated by

Douglas Hall
A.R.C.A.

Selected by Karen Sullivan

BROCKHAMPTON PRESS

Contact with children teaches us sincerity, simplicity, the habit of living in the present hour, the present action.

Father Alexander Elchaninov, *Diary of a Russian Priest*

A faithful friend is a strong defence: and he that hath found such a one hath found a treasure.

Ecclesiastes, VI:14

Love is only chatter,
Friends are all that matter.

G. Burgess, *Willy and the Lady*

What is thine is mine, and all mine is thine.

Plautus

Should auld acquaintance be forgot,
And never brought to mind?
Should auld acquaintance be forgot,
And days o' auld lang syne.
Robert Burns, 'Auld Lang Syne'

A friend is, as it were, a second self.

Cicero

A thought which does not result in an action is nothing much, and an action which does not proceed from a thought is nothing at all.

Georges Bernanos

Thou wert my guide, philosopher, and friend.

Alexander Pope, *An Essay on Man*

But if the while I think on thee, dear friend,
All losses are restored and sorrows end.

William Shakespeare, *Sonnets*

Not what we give, but what we share,
For the gift without the giver is bare.

James Russell Lowell

Loyal friendship
Pure and true
Such is what
I feel for you.
Victorian rhyme

I awoke this morning with devout thanksgiving for
all my friends.
Ralph Waldo Emerson

In prosperity our friends know us;
in adversity we know our friends.
John C. Collins

Hold a true friend with both hands.
Nigerian proverb

But words are things, and
a small drop of ink,
Falling like dew, upon a thought, produces
That which makes thousands, perhaps millions,
think.
Lord Byron

No distance breaks the ties
of blood; brothers are
brothers evermore.
John Keble

Here is a little forest,
Whose leaf is ever green;
Here is a brighter garden,
Where not a frost has been;
In its unfading flowers
I hear the bright bee hum;
Prithee my brother,
Into my garden come.
Emily Dickinson

The greatest grace of a gift, perhaps, is that it
anticipates and admits no return.
Henry Wadsworth Longfellow

Oh the comfort, the inexpressible comfort of feeling safe with a person, having neither to weigh thoughts nor measure words, but pouring them all right out, just as they are, chaff and grain together; certain that a faithful hand will take and sift them, keep what is worth keeping, and then with the breath of kindness, blow the rest away.

Dinah Craik

You will find as you look back upon your life that the moments when you have really loved are the moments when you have done things in the spirit of love.

Henry Drummond

While you have a thing it can be taken from you . . . but when you give it, you have given it. No robber can take it from you. It is yours then for ever when you have given it. It will be yours always. That is to give.

James Joyce

Grief can take care of itself, but to get the full value of a joy you must have somebody to divide it with.

Mark Twain

Come in the evening, or come in the morning;
Come when you're looked for, or come
without warning.
Thomas Osborne Davis, *The Welcome*

✦

Kindness is a language the dumb can speak, and
the deaf can hear and understand.
Christian Bovée

✦

Unselfish and noble actions are the most radiant
pages in the biography of souls.
Thames

✦

Happiness seems made to be shared.
Jean Racine

Thank God we're living in a country where the sky's the limit, the stores are open late and you can shop in bed thanks to television.

Joan Rivers

Friendship! now I love the feeling,
Sweetly soothing to the mind,
When o'er my soul sweet mem'ry stealing,
Leaves a holy calm behind.
Then to Fancy's eye appearing,
Forms beloved, tho' distant far,
Wake affection's glowing feeling,
Silence very passion's jar.

Anonymous

It is normal to give away a little of one's life in
order not to lose it all.
Albert Camus

I thank God far more for friends than for my
daily bread — for friendship is the bread of
my heart.
Mary Mitford

When friends ask, there is no tomorrow, only now.
Alexander Drey

Her unselfishness came in pretty small packages
well wrapped.
F. Scott Fitzgerald

They say late thanks are ever best.
Francis Bacon, Letter to Robert, Lord Cecil

There is something in the unselfish and self-
sacrificing love of a brute, which goes directly to
the heart of him who has had frequent occasion to
test the paltry friendship and gossamer fidelity of
mere Man.
Edgar Allan Poe

The best thing to give to:
Your enemy is forgiveness;
An opponent, tolerance;
A friend, your heart;
Your child, a good example;
Yourself, respect;
All men, charity.
F. M. Balfour

Little deeds of kindness, little words of love,
Help to make earth happy, like the heaven above.
Julia Carney, 'Little Things'

Freely you have received, freely give.
Matthew, X:8

You're my friend,
So I brought you this book.
I give you this flower;
I hand you my hand.

John Marvin

Actions, not words, are the true criteria of the
attachment of friends.
George Washington

He does good to himself,
who does good to his friend.
Erasmus

Do all the good you can,
By all the means you can,
In all the ways you can,
In all the places you can,
At all the times you can,
To all the people you can,
As long as ever you can.
John Wesley

No metaphysician ever felt the deficiency of
language so much as the grateful.
Charles Caleb Colton

The best moments of a visit are those which again
and again postpone its close.
Jean Paul Richter

Thank God for friends, more prized as
years increase,
Who, as possessions fail our hearts and hands,
Become the boon supreme, than gold and lands
More precious. Let all else, if must be, cease;
But, Lord of Lire, I pray on me bestow
The gifts of friends to share the way I go.
Thomas Curtis Clark

It is only the great-hearted who can be true
friends; the mean and the cowardly can never
know what true friendship is.

Charles Kingsley

It is futile to judge a kind deed by its motives.
Kindness can become its own motive. We are made
kind by being kind.

Eric Hoffer

Have you had a kindness shown?
Pass it on;
'Twas not given for thee alone,
Pass it on;
Let it travel down the years,
Let it wipe another's tears,
'Till in Heaven the deed appears —
Pass it on.
Henry Burton

If you stop to be kind, you must swerve often
from your path.
Mary Webb

Be assured when you see a tear on a cheek
a heart is touched.
Anonymous

It is a terrible thing, this kindness that human beings do not lose. Terrible because when we are finally naked in the dark and cold, it is all we have. We who are so rich, so full of strength, wind up with that small change. We have nothing else to give.

Ursula K. Le Guin

Were there no God, we would be in this glorious world with grateful hearts and no one to thank.
Christina Rossetti

⬛

Being good is just a matter of temperament in the end.
Iris Murdoch

⬛

I breathed a song into the air,
It fell to earth, I know now where . . .
And the song, from beginning to end,
I found again in the heart of a friend.
Henry Wadsworth Longfellow

I thank my God every time I remember you.

Philippians, 1:3

The cosy fire is bright and gay,
The merry kettle boils away
And hums a cheerful song.
I sing the saucer and the cup;
Pray, Mary, fill the tea pot up,
And do not make it strong.

William Cowper, 'The Poets at Tea'

'Stay' is a charming word in a friend's
vocabulary.

Louisa May Alcott

No one is so rich that he does not need another's help; no one so poor as not to be useful in some way to his fellow man.
Pope Leo XIII

Those who bring sunshine to the lives of others cannot keep it from themselves.
J. M. Barrie

His courtesy was somewhat extravagant. He would write and thank people who wrote to thank him for wedding presents and when he encountered anyone as punctilious as himself the correspondence ended only with death.

Evelyn Waugh

I have learned that to have a good friend is the purest of all God's gifts, for it is a love that has no exchange of payment.

Frances Farmer

Greater love hath no man than this, that a man
lay down his life for his friends.

John, XV:13

Ⓧ

I do detest everything which is not
perfectly mutual.

Lord Byron

Ⓧ

Don't walk in front of me,
I may not follow.
Don't walk behind me,
I may not lead.
Walk beside me
And just be my friend.

Albert Camus

For this relief
much thanks.
William Shakespeare,
Hamlet

The only gift is a portion
of thyself.
Ralph Waldo Emerson

The smallest act of kindness is worth more
than the grandest intention.
Proverb

You must give some time to your fellow men.
Even if it's a little thing, do something for others —
something for which you get no pay but the
privilege of doing it.
Albert Schweitzer

Giving presents is a talent; to know what a person
wants, to know when and how to get it, to give it
lovingly and well. Unless a character possesses
this talent there is no moment more annihilating
to ease than that in which a present is received
and given.
Pamela Glenconner

Beggar that I am, I am even poor in thanks.
William Shakespeare, *Hamlet*

They seemed to come suddenly upon happiness
as if they had surprised a butterfly in the
winter woods.
Edith Wharton

A friend is what the heart needs all the time.
Henry van Dyke

We have been friends together
in sunshine and shade.
Caroline Norton

A cheque or credit card, a Gucci bag strap,
anything of value will do. Give as you live.
Jesse Jackson

You bring sunshine to my rainy day.

American proverb

The fool saith, I have no friends, I have no thanks for all my good deeds, and they that eat my bread speak evil of me.

Ecclesiastes, XX:16

Let us be thankful for the fools. But for them the rest of us could not succeed.

Mark Twain

Ever since Eve gave Adam the apple,
there has been a misunderstanding between
the sexes about gifts.
Nan Robertson

'Presents', I often say,
'endear absents'.
Charles Lamb, *Essays of Elia*

Friends are necessary to a happy life. When friendship deserts us we are as lonely and helpless as a ship, left by the tide high upon the shore. When friendship returns to us, it is as though the tide came back, gave us buoyancy and freedom, and opened to us the wide places of the world.

Harry Emerson Fosdick

Down on your knees,
And thank heaven, fasting, for a good man's love.

William Shakespeare, *As You Like It*

My muse and I must you of duty greet
With thanks and wishes, wishing thankfully.

Sir Philip Sidney, 'Sonnet'

Thank you for thinking up the little things you do, and then doing them.

Anonymous

Ah yet, ere I descend to the grave
May I a small house and a large garden have;
And a few friends, and many books, both true,
Both wise, and both delightful too!

Comte de Bussy-Rabutin

Nothing costs so much as what is given us.

Thomas Fuller, *Gnomologia*

The manner of giving is worth more than the gift.

Pierre Corneille

Such thanks
As fits a king's remembrance.

William Shakespeare, *Hamlet*

May the Lord bless you and take care of you;
May the Lord be kind and gracious to you;
May the Lord look on you and give you peace.

The Priestly Blessing

The Family is the Country of the heart. There is an angel in the Family who, by the mysterious influence of grace, of sweetness, and of love, renders the fulfilment of duties less wearisome, sorrows less bitter. The only pure joys unmixed with sadness which it is given to man to taste upon earth are, thanks to this angel, the joys of the Family.

Giuseppe Mazzini

Everything that God has created is good; nothing is to be rejected, but everything is to be received with a prayer of thanks.

Paul's First Letters to Timothy

God gives us our relatives — thank God we can choose our friends.

Ethel Watts Mumford

This little book is just
for you
To thank you for the
things you do.
Anonymous

Maybe the only thing
worse than having to
give gratitude
constantly . . .
is having to accept it.
William Faulkner

Rejoice in the Lord, O ye righteous;
For it becometh well the just to be thankful.
Psalms

❖

For Fortune hath kept her promise
In granting me my most desire.
Sir Thomas Wyatt,
'The Lover Rejoiceth the Enjoying of His Lover'

❖

To be more happy I dare not aspire.
John Dryden, *The Maiden Queen*

❖

Gratitude — the meanest and most snivelling
attribute in the world.
Dorothy Parker

I can never thank you enough because you have been there, you have stood beside me, you have propped me up, and let me down gently. You have rebuilt me and made me strong. I am a tower of your thoughts and care. Thank you.

Greeting card inscription

I can no other answer make but thanks
And thanks, and ever thanks.

William Shakespeare, *Twelfth Night*

I thank the goodness and the grace
Which on my birth have smiled.

Ann and Jane Taylor, *Hymns for Infant Minds*

I'm grateful for the past.
William Congreve, *False Though She Be*

＊

A man's indebtedness . . . is not virtue; his
repayment is. Virtue begins when he dedicates
himself actively to the job of gratitude.
Ruth Benedict

＊

When I'm not thank'd at all, I'm thank'd enough,
I've done my duty, and I've done no more.
Henry Fielding, *Tom Thumb the Great*

＊

For what is love itself, for the one we love best? —
an enfolding of immeasurable cares which yet are
better than any joys outside our love.
George Eliot, *Daniel Deronda*

One of the effects of a safe and civilised life
is an immense oversensitiveness which makes all
the primary emotions somewhat disgusting.
Generosity is as painful as meanness, gratitude as
hateful as ingratitude.
George Orwell

❖

Isn't life a terrible thing, thank God!
Dylan Thomas, *Under Milk Wood*

❖

Friendships begin with liking or gratitude . . .
George Eliot, *Daniel Deronda*

❖

Gratitude is the most exquisite form of courtesy.
Jacques Maritain

Nothing you do for children is ever wasted. They seem not to notice us, hovering, averting our eyes, and they seldom offer thanks, but what we do for them is never wasted.

Garrison Keillor, *Leaving Home*

Charity never humiliated him who profited from it, nor ever bound him by the chains of gratitude, since it was not to him but to God that the gift was made.

Antoine de Saint-Exupéry

There are minds so impatient of inferiority that their gratitude is a species of revenge, and they return benefits, not because recompense is a pleasure, but because obligation is a pain.

Samuel Johnson

Gifts must affect the receiver to the point of shock.
Walter Benjamin

I come to be grateful at last for
a little thing.
Alfred, Lord Tennyson, *Maud*

Do not do unto others as you would that they
should do unto you. Their tastes may not be
the same.
George Bernard Shaw

Why is it no one ever sent me yet
One perfect limousine, do you suppose?
Ah no, it's always just my luck to get
One perfect rose.
Dorothy Parker

Generosity lies less in giving much than in
giving at the right moment.
Jean de la Bruyère

There is sublime thieving in all giving.
Someone gives us all he has and we are his.
Eric Hoffer

Then — dear one — you have been the blessing
of my life.
George Eliot, *The Mill on the Floss*

Camerado, I give you my hand!
I give you my love more precious than money,
I give you myself before preaching or law;
Will you give me yourself?
Walt Whitman

People who think they're generous to a fault
usually think that's their only fault.
Sydney J. Harris

It is always so pleasant to be generous,
though very vexatious to pay debts.
Ralph Waldo Emerson

Give all thou canst; high Heaven rejects the lore
Of nicely-calculated less or more.
William Wordsworth

A grateful mind
By owing owes not, but still pays, at once
Indebted and discharged.
John Milton, 'Paradise Lost'

I hate ingratitude more in a man
Than lying, vainness, babbling drunkenness,
Or any taint of vice whose strong corruption
Inhabits our frail blood.
William Shakespeare, *Twelfth Night*

Thank you very much indeed,
River, for your waving reed;
Hollyhocks, for
budding knobs;
Foxgloves, for
your velvet fobs;
Pansies, for your
silky cheeks;
Chaffinches, for
singing beaks . . .
Norman Gale, 'Thanks'

What am I to say to you? You saved me last night.
Oscar Wilde, *Lady Windermere's Fan*

In most of mankind gratitude is merely a secret
hope of further favours.
François, Duc de la Rochefoucauld

While the bright sun doth shine
I'll ne'er forget thee.

Victorian saying

◈

Joy is prayer — Joy is strength — Joy is love —
Joy is a net of love by which you can catch souls.
God loves a cheerful giver. She gives most who
gives with joy. The best way to show our gratitude
to God and the people is to accept everything with
joy. A joyful heart is the inevitable result of a
heart burning with love. Never let anything so fill
you with sorrow as to make you forget the joy of
the Christ risen.

Mother Teresa

◈

Two souls in one, two hearts into one heart . . .

Du Bartas

One can never pay in gratitude; one can only pay
'in kind' somewhere else in life.
Anne Morrow Lindbergh

Behold, I do not give lectures or a little charity,
When I give I give myself.
Walt Whitman

Too many have dispensed with generosity in order
to practise charity.
Albert Camus, *The Fall*

When turkey's on the table laid
And good things I may scan
I'm thankful that I wasn't made
A vegetarian.
Edgar A. Guest

The art of acceptance is the art of making someone
who has done you a small favour wish that he
might have done you a greater one.
Russell Lynes

Our charity begins at home,
And most ends where it begins.
Horace Smith, *Horace in London*

◈

We must take care to indulge only in such
generosity as will help our friends and hurt no
one — for nothing is generous, if it is not at the
same time just.
Cicero

◈

Acknowledgements:

The Publishers wish to thank everyone who gave permission to reproduce the quotes in this book. Every effort has been made to contact the copyright holders, but in the event that an oversight has occurred, the publishers would be delighted to rectify any omissions in future editions of this book. *Good News Study Bible,* published by Thomas Nelson, 1986, extracts reprinted with their kind permission; James Joyce reprinted courtesy of The Bodley Head and Random House, Inc.; J. M. Barrie © Great Ormond Street Children's Hospital, reprinted with their kind permission; Dylan Thomas, *Under Milkwood,* published by J. M. Dent, reprinted courtesy of David Higham Associates; Dorothy Parker quotes from *The Best of Dorothy Parker,* first published by Methuen in 1952, reprinted by Gerald Duckworth & Co., © Dorothy Parker, 1956, 1957, 1958, 1959, renewed; George Bernard Shaw, reprinted courtesy of the Society of Authors on behalf of the Estate of George Bernard Shaw; *Leaving Home,* by Garrison Keillor, reprinted courtesy of Faber & Faber and Viking Penguin; Joan Rivers and others quoted in *1911 Best Things Anybody Ever Said,* by Robert Byrne, published by Ballantine Books © 1988 Robert Byrne, reprinted by permission of Random House, Inc., New York, and Random House of Canada Limited, Toronto; *Penguin Book of Japanese Verse,* translated by Geoffrey Bownas and Anthony Thwaite, published by Penguin 1964, and reprinted with their permission.